Heinz
Baked
Beanz

hamlyn

First published in Great Britain in 2006 by Hamlyn,
a division of Octopus Publishing Group Ltd,
2–4 Heron Quays, London E14 4JP

ISBN-13: 978-0-600-61599-6
ISBN-10: 0-600-61599-5

A CIP catalogue record for this book is available from the British Library

Printed and bound in Italy

10 9 8 7 6 5 4 3 2 1

the bean,
the superbean

Contents

Heinz
– a canned history

Beanz count among the nation's favourite things and everyone has their own ideas about how to eat them: straight from the can, poured piping hot over toast or stuffed into a baked potato. This short history of Beanz outlines how they earned a place in our hearts and on our plates, from their small beginnings to their prominent role in food history.

Above Beanz Meanz Heinz outdoor poster, 1966.

small beginnings

Baked Beanz have a long history and we have Henry J. Heinz to thank for our contemporary take on this venerable food. Born on 11 October 1844 near Pittsburgh, Pennsylvania, Henry began his career in the food business before he'd reached his teens. While other boys were still climbing trees and getting grubby, Henry was busy helping his mother Anna sell produce from the family's kitchen garden. This entrepreneurial mother-and-son team progressed to selling jars of homemade horseradish sauce to local grocers and neighbours. Despite the fact that food processing was still in its infancy in young Henry's day, there were familiar brands available to consumers and it wasn't easy for a new product to get noticed on the shelves. Showing great commercial acumen, Henry highlighted the fact that their horseradish sauce wasn't bulked out with filling agents and other nasty ingredients by bottling the sauce in clear glass jars, and it wasn't long before Pittsburgh's canny shoppers discovered the difference in taste and quality.

Above The founder Henry John Heinz (1844–1919), 1886.

boom, bust and boom again

This philosophy of openness and honesty about the food he produced was central to the young entrepreneur. Henry realized that fancy packaging didn't fool people – they appreciated good quality food, and he spotted a huge gap in the market for his range of pickles, sauces and baked beans. In 1869 Henry went into business with a friend and they launched the company Heinz & Noble.

Production began in earnest from the family home, with a couple of employees preparing and bottling the horseradish sauce in the family kitchen. Baked beans were added to the repertoire and business was good, with word-of-mouth recommendations and clever marketing ensuring that Heinz & Noble products took pride of place in many a Pennsylvanian pantry. However, success was short-lived as recession hit the USA in 1875 and the small company, like countless others, went bankrupt.

Undeterred by bankruptcy and recession, Henry immediately scraped together the funds to start again and this time only the Heinz name appeared on the labels of these superior sauces, pickles and baked beans. As before, once the products had been sampled, they sold themselves and the demand grew for Henry's tasty range of foods that livened up boring meals.

Above A Heinz Baked Beans can from the 1890s.

Above Henry J. Heinz visiting Fortnum & Mason, 1886.

and the result was the decision by the Head of Purchasing to take all of the baked beans.

1898

Thus began Britain's love affair with Heinz. Encouraged by this initial success, Henry decided to establish a London base for the company. A temporary base was found near Tower Bridge and operations eventually moved to permanent premises on Farringdon Road in 1898. From here, Heinz products were imported and distributed around the country.

conquering Britain

1886

Not content with revolutionizing the American dinner table, Henry felt it was time to take his products on a trip abroad. In 1886 the Heinz family embarked on a European tour, with Henry taking a stack of his baked beans. The stay included a two-week stopover in London, where Henry famously visited Fortnum & Mason. It was typical of Henry to go straight to the most esteemed food outlet in London to promote his wares. However, this dogged self-belief paid off

international Heinz

1919

Heinz products proved so popular that the British side of the business was registered as a British company, and plans were made to build a food production plant in the UK. Sadly, Henry J. Heinz never realized his dream of an international Heinz company as he died in 1919, a few years before the first food production plant was opened in Britain. His son Howard took over the business and continued to drive the company forward, while sticking doggedly to those all-important principles that his father had established many years before.

bean, mushroom and brie-filled pancakes

Serves 4
Preparation time 20 minutes
Cooking time 25–30 minutes

pancakes
75 g (3 oz) plain flour
1 egg
125 ml (4 fl oz) milk
15 g (½ oz) butter, melted
2 tablespoons chopped basil leaves
olive oil spray, for greasing
salt and pepper

bean filling
415 g (13½ oz) can Heinz Baked Beanz
1 tablespoon light olive oil
2 onions, chopped
2 garlic cloves, chopped
275 g (9 oz) field mushrooms,
     roughly chopped
125 g (4 oz) brie cheese,
     cut into 1 cm (½ inch) cubes
butter, for greasing
2 tablespoons grated Parmesan cheese
mixed salad, to serve

1 Make the pancakes. Sift the flour into a large bowl and season with salt and pepper. Make a well in the centre of the flour and whisk in the egg and milk, gradually incorporating the flour until the whole mixture is smooth and has the consistency of single cream. Beat in the melted butter and basil.

2 Heat a medium-sized, nonstick frying pan over medium heat and spray with a little oil. Pour in enough batter to make a thin pancake, swirling the pan to get an even coverage. Cook for 2 minutes or until the pancake is lightly browned underneath. Use a spatula to flip over the pancake and cook for a further 1 minute. Repeat to make 4 pancakes in all, stacking them between layers of baking parchment.

3 Make the filling. Heat the oil in a large, nonstick frying pan and cook the onion over medium-high heat for 3–4 minutes or until soft. Add the garlic and mushrooms and continue to cook for 5 minutes or until cooked. Remove the pan from the heat and stir in the **Heinz Baked Beanz** and brie.

4 Divide the bean filling among the pancakes, rolling up each one as you fill it. Place the filled pancakes in a lightly buttered, shallow ovenproof dish and sprinkle over the Parmesan. Place the dish under a preheated medium-high grill and cook the pancakes for 4–5 minutes until they are golden and heated through. Serve warm with mixed salad.

bean, courgette and herb frittata

Serves 6
Preparation time 15 minutes
Cooking time 25–30 minutes

200 g (7 oz) can Heinz Baked Beanz
2 tablespoons olive oil
1 red onion, cut into segments
2 courgettes, cut into 1 cm (½ inch) slices
6 eggs, lightly beaten
3 tablespoons chopped oregano
3 tablespoons grated Parmesan cheese
pepper
rocket salad, to serve

1 Heat 1 tablespoon oil in a nonstick frying pan and cook the onion for 5 minutes or until it is soft. Transfer to a plate and leave to one side. Heat the remaining oil in the pan and cook the courgettes for 6–7 minutes. Spoon the **Heinz Baked Beanz** over the courgettes and add the cooked onion.

2 Beat together the eggs and oregano and season well with pepper. Pour the eggs into the pan and cook over medium heat for 10–15 minutes, gently pulling in the cooked edges with a fork every now and then to allow uncooked egg to run to the sides. When the frittata is golden underneath and almost cooked on top, scatter it with Parmesan and place under a preheated grill for 5 minutes until the top is set and golden.

3 Slide the frittata on to a serving plate or board and cut it into 6 wedges. Serve with a rocket salad.

spicy tomato and bean soup

Serves 4
Preparation time 10 minutes
Cooking time 30 minutes

415 g (13½ oz) can Heinz Baked Beanz
2 tablespoons vegetable oil
1 onion, roughly chopped
125 g (4 oz) celery stick, chopped
1 garlic clove, crushed
2 teaspoons dried mixed herbs
1 teaspoon dried crushed chilli
400 g (13 oz) can chopped tomatoes
600 ml (1 pint) vegetable stock

to serve
4 tablespoons soured cream
toasted bread

1 Heat the oil in a heavy-based pan. Add the onion, celery, garlic, mixed herbs and chilli and cook over medium heat for 5 minutes.

2 Add the tomatoes, **Heinz Baked Beanz** and stock to the pan, bring to the boil, cover and simmer for 25 minutes.

3 Serve the soup in warm bowls topped with a swirl of soured cream and accompanied with chunks of bread.

the birth of the bean

Although we consider beans to be an essential storecupboard staple, they haven't always been so quick and easy to prepare. In the days before cans were available, everything was prepared from scratch, meaning beans weren't as convenient as they are today.

the first baked bean

When the early pioneers made their way slowly across the American West in wagon trains to find a better life for themselves, conditions were notoriously tough.

People lived on the trails in very basic conditions, with a limited stock of food supplies. Meals were dull and repetitive, and could only be made from ingredients easily transported by wagon. A lack of refrigeration meant that most foodstuffs were dried or preserved products intended to last for the duration of journeys that took many months.

Beans were therefore an ideal solution and became a popular favourite with the pioneers for their versatility and durability.

Above Beans on the range.

meals on wheels

Flour, sugar, coffee and beans were the staples of the pioneers' daily diet, with cured meat and milk from their animals adding an occasional element of variety. Meals needed to be cooked quickly over a campfire. Dried beans kept indefinitely and, once prepared, provided a filling and nutritious meal. The dried beans were soaked overnight or while the wagon was on the move during the day. Cured meat was often added to the pot while the beans were cooking.

the first celebrity chefs

As settled communities were established, cattle ranches sprang up and the cowboy culture emerged. Meals had to be nutritious, plentiful and easy to prepare. The chuckwagon was born – a kind of early mobile catering van run by a dedicated cook. Two Texans, Oliver Loving and Charles Goodnight, are said to have come up with the idea of the chuckwagon, and it turned out to be a sensible solution to the problem of feeding very hungry men on the move.

Above Cowboy children's promotion, 1950s.

Once again, beans played an important role. Compact and easy to transport when dried, they would be used as the basis for most meals. The chuckwagon would arrive before the hungry cowboys so that the cook had time to prepare the food. The men would arrive to the smell of a hot meal bubbling away over the campfire.

the bean revolution

The original dish of beans baked in a sauce is credited to Native Americans. They slow-cooked haricot beans in clay pots with maple syrup and bear fat. The recipe was passed on to colonists and evolved to become the famous Boston Baked Beans. This meal was traditionally served on Saturday evenings throughout New England, to conform with the religious tradition of not cooking on the Sabbath (Saturday night to Sunday night). The beans would be set to cook slowly on Saturday morning and families could then sit down in the evening to enjoy a hot meal together.

in the can

Canned baked beans were first produced by the Heinz company in Pittsburgh in 1895. Baked beans found their way on to British tables nine years later when Heinz began exporting their products. At first, baked beans were seen as a luxury item due to their price and limited availability, but when the first cans of British-made baked beans came off the production line at the Harlesden factory in 1928, Heinz was able to slash the price and make them an everyday option.

Above North of England press advertisement, 1905–1906.

wartime beans

The Second World War meant hard times and food shortages for everyone. Rationing put paid to fancy meals and luxury foodstuffs, so housewives had to learn to be creative with ingredients while providing healthy meals. Far from taking a backseat during the difficult war years, Heinz pressed on with advertising and baked beans became the perfect wartime food. They could be purchased with ration books and presented people with a nutritious storecupboard staple. In fact, baked beans were classified as an 'essential food' by the British Ministry of Food as part of the wartime rationing system. During the lean post-war years baked beans continued to provide much-needed nutrition.

the Swinging Sixties

During the sixties one of the most recognized advertising slogans of all time – Beanz Meanz Heinz – was introduced. This ad ran in various forms for over 22 years and became synonymous with Heinz Baked Beanz – not bad, considering it was written in a pub in Mornington Crescent, London, over a couple of pints of beer.

the 1990s onwards

By the 1990s, beans were being sold in more than 60 countries around the world and had even reached plates in China and Russia. Today, in response to concerns about salt and sugar levels, beans are even healthier, with 50% less salt and 25% less sugar. Henry J. Heinz once said, 'Quality is to product what character is to man', and his dedication to producing the very best has resulted in a food that has captured the hearts and stomachs of many generations.

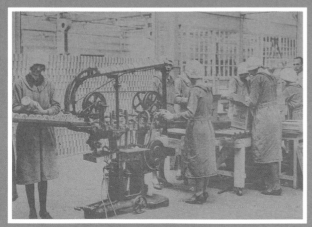

Above Labelling and packing, Harlesden factory, 1930.

maple and smoked bacon beanz with damper rolls

Serves 4
Preparation time 30 minutes
Cooking time 20 minutes

damper rolls
200 g (7 oz) butter
300 g (10 oz) self-raising flour
1 teaspoon salt
150 ml (6 fl oz) milk
2 garlic cloves, crushed
2 tablespoons chopped basil

maple and smoked bacon beanz
4 x 200 g (7 oz) cans Heinz Baked Beanz
1 onion, chopped
1 teaspoon Spanish smoked paprika
  (pimenton)
250 g (8 oz) smoked bacon rashers,
  cut into large pieces
3 tablespoons maple syrup
sprigs of parsley, to garnish

1 Make the rolls. Cut 125 g (4 oz) butter into dice. Place the flour in a bowl, add the salt and diced butter and rub in with your fingertips until the mixture resembles fine breadcrumbs. Add the milk and bring the mixture together until it forms a soft dough.

2 Mix the remaining butter with the garlic and basil and leave to one side. Divide the dough into 12 equal pieces and press each into a small disc. Divide the herb butter into 12 and put a piece in the centre of each dough disc. Gather up the sides of each disc, making the dough into a ball and enclosing the butter. Place each roll, smooth side up, on a lightly greased baking sheet, leaving space for each one to rise slightly. Bake in a preheated oven, 200°C (400°F), Gas Mark 6, for 10–15 minutes or until golden brown.

3 Make the bean mixture. Preheat a nonstick frying pan and cook the onion, paprika and bacon together for 3–4 minutes or until the bacon is starting to crisp. Stir in the maple syrup and bring to the boil. Continue to stir for a minute until the syrup caramelizes. Add the **Heinz Baked Beanz** and 100 ml (3½ fl oz) water and bring to the boil. Serve the beans, garnished with a sprig of parsley, with the warm damper rolls.

the Heinz factory

The fact that Heinz has grown from the time it first began trading proves its ability to adapt and change according to times and tastes. Sauces have been tweaked, products updated and new ranges introduced to meet demand.

stepping up production

After the devastation of the Second World War, there was even more call for Heinz products as Europe opened up and more people got a taste for these flavoursome sauces, soups and beans. Demand so outstripped production that the Harlesden factory couldn't keep up, so the search was on for a new site. In 1959, Kitt Green in Lancashire opened and is, to this day, the largest food processing plant in Europe, spread over an astonishing 56 acres and producing 85 million cases of food a year! It has also given the nearby town of Wigan the title of 'Baked Beans Centre of the World'.

an exact science

Food processing has come on a long way since the days when Henry J. Heinz made horseradish sauce with his mother in their kitchen. Nowadays, food technologists examine every single aspect of the baked beans, from the raw ingredients through to the finished can. The beans go through a number of changes as they are cooked, cooled and then packaged, and it is important to understand how each process affects the final product. The aim is to

Above Wigan Railway Station, 1959.

make the beans taste great and be as nutritious as possible. Each new baked bean product passes through the rigorous Heinz Test Kitchens at Kitt Green, which monitor everything from the bean texture, vitamin levels and even the consistency of the sauce!

a family affair

Heinz is renowned as a good employer. During the company's first years of trading, its employees were treated like family and hard work was rewarded with an enviable range of benefits. One of the more unusual perks included a weekly manicure for all ladies who handled food (unfortunately, this is no longer offered!). Staff changing rooms were a talking point, featuring marble basins and hot running water, a luxury that many people would not have enjoyed at home. Heinz was among the first companies to introduce holiday pay for its employees, which meant that people could afford to take a break with their families.

Since Heinz began producing beans, sauces have been tweaked, products updated and new ranges introduced to reflect the changing attitudes towards food, nutrition, health and flavours but the core tastes, values and ideals of the original company remain firmly in place. Today, Heinz produces a staggering 3,000 products and sells them in more than 200 countries. So, wherever you are in the world, you can be sure that you are never too far from a can of Heinz Baked Beanz!

Above A Heinz employee enjoying a manicure.

portobello mushrooms with beanz and grilled haloumi cheese

Serves 4 as a starter
or 2 as a main course
Preparation time 10 minutes
Cooking time 20 minutes

415 g (13½ oz) can Heinz Baked Beanz
4 large portobello mushrooms
2 garlic cloves, finely chopped
4 tablespoons chopped mixed fresh herbs
(such as thyme, rosemary,
chives and parsley)
6 tablespoons olive oil
few drops of balsamic vinegar
8 thin slices of haloumi cheese
pepper

to serve
75 g (3 oz) rocket leaves
1 pear, cored and sliced
25 g (1 oz) freshly grated Parmesan cheese

1 Remove the stems from the mushrooms and place them, gill sides up, in an ovenproof dish. Sprinkle over half the garlic and herbs and season with pepper. Drizzle with half the oil, place in a preheated oven, 200°C (400°F), Gas Mark 6, and roast for 10–15 minutes or until cooked through.

2 Mix the **Heinz Baked Beanz** with a few drops of balsamic vinegar and heat through gently. Spoon the beans over the cooked mushrooms and arrange the slices of haloumi over the beans. Scatter over the reserved garlic and herbs and drizzle with the remaining oil. Place the dish under a preheated high grill and cook for 2–3 minutes or until golden brown.

3 Place the mushrooms on individual serving dishes and serve with a rocket, pear and Parmesan salad.

bean nachos with melted cheese

Serves 4
Preparation time 10 minutes
Cooking time 10 minutes

415 g (13½ oz) can Heinz Baked Beanz
230 g (7½ oz) tortilla chips
1 avocado
200 g (7 oz) cherry tomatoes, halved
125 g (4 oz) Cheddar cheese, grated
1 large green chilli, finely sliced
pepper

1 Place the tortilla chips in a large, heatproof serving dish or 4 smaller serving dishes.

2 Spoon the **Heinz Baked Beanz** over the chips. Peel the avocado, remove the stone and cut the flesh into dice. Arrange the tomatoes and avocado pieces over the beans, scatter over the cheese and top with the sliced chilli.

3 Season well with pepper and bake in a preheated oven, 200°C (400°F), Gas Mark 6, for 10 minutes or until the cheese is bubbling and the tops of the nachos have browned.

cheesy bean and beef fajitas

Serves 4
Preparation time 20 minutes
Cooking time about 11 minutes

415 g (13½ oz) can Heinz Baked Beanz
2 sirloin steaks, each about 250 g (8 oz)
35 g (1½ oz) fajita seasoning mix
grated rind of 1 lime
2 tablespoons light olive oil
1 red onion, sliced
1 green pepper, cored, deseeded
   and sliced
1 yellow pepper, cored, deseeded
   and sliced
8 small flour tortillas, warmed
50 g (2 oz) Cheddar cheese, grated
8 tablespoons soured cream

1 Sprinkle the steaks on both sides with half the seasoning mix and lime rind. Brush with a little of the oil and leave to one side. Put the onion and sliced peppers in a bowl and toss with the remaining seasoning mix and lime rind. Heat a griddle pan to hot and cook the steaks for 2–3 minutes on each side.

2 Heat the remaining oil in a nonstick frying pan and cook the onion and peppers for 5 minutes over medium-high heat until they are cooked through. Add the **Heinz Baked Beanz** to the pan and stir to mix. Bring to the boil and remove from the heat. Cut the meat into thin strips. Place spoonfuls of the bean mixture in the warmed tortillas, top with grated cheese and slices of beef and drizzle with soured cream, then wrap and serve.

the life of a bean

Heinz Baked Beanz are made using navy beans – a variety of haricot from the Phaseolus species. Navy beans are so-called because they were standard American Navy fare from the mid-19th century.

Only the cream of the navy bean crop makes it through the rigorous testing imposed on every bean. Crops are grown in Michigan then shipped across to the Heinz UK factory in Wigan for selection and canning. The UK factory wades through an incredible one thousand tonnes of navy beans each week!

making the grade

Only the best navy beans are used in Heinz Baked Beanz. When they arrive in Wigan the selection process continues. Beans that are too hard or oversized are rejected immediately. A machine like a giant sieve separates out the smaller, more tender beans, and those allowed through are then rinsed in water to get rid of any residue or fibres. They are washed again and cooked briefly in hot

water to soften them and ensure maximum taste. But that's not it! To eliminate the possibility of any rogue bean making the grade, every bean is further scrutinized under a laser beam. Cracked or oversized intruders are swiftly removed by a blast of air aimed precisely at the culprit. Those that survive are eligible to be turned into Heinz Baked Beanz.

the secret is in the sauce

The recipe for the tomato sauce used in Heinz Baked Beanz is one of the world's most closely guarded culinary secrets. It is reputed that only four people at any one time know the recipe and keeping it secret is taken extremely seriously. If you are one of the many people who believes that no other baked beans taste quite like Heinz, then you will appreciate why the information is highly classified. We can reveal that special varieties of tomato are grown just for the sauce and these are combined with a range of spices and herbs to produce the distinctive rich flavour that is synonymous with Heinz Baked Beanz – but we can say no more than that!

Above The founder's grandson, Henry J. Heinz II (1908–1987) at Kitt Green, 1959.

packing power

Once the beans and sauce have been combined, the cans are sealed shut using a special process called seaming. Henry Heinz was against the use of any artificial preservatives – a progressive stance that placed him well ahead of his time – and this method of sealing the cans means such preservatives are unnecessary. To avoid contamination from bacteria the cans are steamed at high temperatures for half an hour and then cooled. Once the labels have been added, the cans are sorted, packed and distributed.

pumpkin, bean and tomato risotto

Serves 4
Preparation time 20 minutes
Cooking time 30 minutes

415 g (13½ oz) can Heinz Baked Beanz
1 tablespoon olive oil
25 g (1 oz) butter
1 onion, finely chopped
325 g (11 oz) pumpkin, peeled, deseeded
    and cut into 1 cm (½ inch) cubes
2 garlic cloves, chopped
275 g (9 oz) arborio rice
125 ml (4 fl oz) white wine
750 ml (1¼ pints) hot vegetable stock
3 tomatoes, skinned, deseeded
    and chopped
3 tablespoons torn basil
pepper

to serve
6 tablespoons grated Parmesan cheese
crusty bread

1 Heat the oil and butter in a large, nonstick frying pan. Add the onion and fry over medium heat for 3–4 minutes or until soft. Stir in the pumpkin and garlic, season with pepper and cook for 8–10 minutes or until the pumpkin starts to soften. Add the rice and stir until it is coated in the butter and juices. Stir in the wine and cook until it has been absorbed by the rice.

2 Add a ladleful of stock to the rice and cook over medium heat, stirring, until the liquid is absorbed. Add another ladleful of stock and continue cooking and stirring for 15–18 minutes or until the rice is tender. You may not need all the stock.

3 Stir in the **Heinz Baked Beanz** and tomatoes, bring to the boil and add the torn basil. Serve the risotto with lots of Parmesan and crusty bread.

what's in a bean?

Convenience foods are not usually celebrated for their nutritional qualities but Heinz founder, Henry J. Heinz, was a bit of a maverick when it came to the key principles behind his best-selling brands. His philosophy of selling wholesome, reasonably priced foods still holds true today.

full of beans

The beans themselves are dried navy or haricot beans, which are related to the lentil, and it may surprise many baked beans fans to learn that their favourite snack is packed full of goodness. This is good news for parents of children who may shun vegetables but happily tuck into anything that is served with some baked beans.

a healthy option

Heinz Baked Beanz are high in fibre and iron, low in fat and cholesterol-free. Recently Heinz has sought to make their beans even more healthy. The salt content in beans has been lowered as standard, and a new reduced sugar and salt version of the traditional recipe has appeared.

the ultimate GI food

The GI (Glycaemic Index) diet may be a relatively recent phenomenon but baked beans have been providing benefits since they were first dropped on to a slice of wholemeal toast. A GI diet works on the principles of eating 'good' or complex carbohydrates, and beans are GI winners.

Nutrition profile

Each 207 g (7 oz) serving of Heinz Baked Beanz (half a standard can) provides the following:

Fibre: 42% RDA; Folate: 20% RDA

Magnesium: 20% RDA; Iron: 20% RDA

Calcium: 10% RDA; Fat : 0.4 g

RDA = recommended daily allowance

heinzbeanz.com

the bean, the superbean.

i am god of fibre.

Above 2004 nutritional advert.

bean and three cheese ravioli

Makes 20 ravioli
Preparation time 50 minutes, plus resting
Cooking time 8–12 minutes

200 g (7 oz) can Heinz Baked Beanz
300 g (10 oz) 00 pasta flour, plus extra for dusting
good pinch of salt
3 large eggs, beaten
150 g (5 oz) ricotta cheese
25 g (1 oz) Parmesan cheese, grated, plus extra to serve
150 g (5 oz) goats' cheese
150 g (5 oz) butter
3 tablespoons chopped sage, plus a few leaves to garnish
grated rind and juice of 1 lemon
pepper
lemon wedges, to serve

1 Sieve the flour into a food processor and add the salt. With the motor running slowly, add the eggs to form a dough. Knead on a clean surface for 5 minutes. Wrap in clingfilm and leave to one side for 30 minutes to relax.

2 Meanwhile, make the filling. Mix together all the cheeses and the **Heinz Baked Beanz**. Season well with pepper. Divide the dough into 4 pieces. Using a pasta machine and starting on the widest setting and going down to the thinnest, roll out the dough into 4 sheets.

3 Place scant heaped teaspoons of the bean filling at 5 cm (2 inch) intervals over 3 sheets of pasta. Brush a little water around the filling to help seal the pasta. Press the remaining sheet over the filling and press down between the mounds. Cut between the mounds to make 8 cm (3 inch) square raviolis. Keep on a lightly floured tea towel until needed. Cook the ravioli in batches in salted boiling water for 2–3 minutes or until the edges of the ravioli are cooked.

4 Melt the butter in a frying pan with the lemon rind and sage. When the butter starts to foam and colour slightly add the lemon juice and remove from the heat. Arrange the ravioli on 4 plates and spoon over the butter sauce. Garnish with extra sage leaves and serve with extra Parmesan and wedges of lemon.

family favourites

Baked beans have always been a food that the whole family can enjoy. They are quick and convenient without the compromises usually associated with convenience foods and many people have grown up eating them.

a good balance

Nutritional information is now widely available and we have a better understanding of the amounts of fresh fruit and vegetables we should be consuming, and the need to limit our intake of fat, sugar and salt. Armed with this information, people are able to make more informed choices about the food they give their families. It is reassuring to know that Heinz Baked Beanz offer the ideal combination of convenience and nutrition.

Above Beanz Meanz Heinz outdoor poster, 1979.

Above Children can't get enough of Heinz Baked Beanz!

hidden nutrition

Beans are a favourite with most children and they have the added bonus of supplying a significant proportion of the body's daily requirements of iron, fibre and magnesium (see page 28). A serving of Baked Beanz (half a 415 g can) also counts as a vegetable portion – a cunningly disguised healthy vegetable that all children will enjoy.

emergency rations

If you have ever been on a family holiday you may well have experienced the phenomenon of packing cans of beans at the expense of clothes and toiletries. Ensuring that the family can have their favourite meal, beans were considered essential for any holiday break. Along with tea bags, Heinz Baked Beanz must surely be the most well-travelled food in the world.

the habit of a lifetime

Of course, once a taste for baked beans is acquired, it will stay with you for life. Those early memories of beans on toast can be re-visited by trying the variations on this classic meal on pages 56–57. It is a well-known fact that baked beans are standard student fare, with economy being a top priority once people leave home. However, it doesn't stop there. When you start working or start a family, baked beans will continue to feature on the menu, providing easy, nutritious meals that save precious time.

chilli bean con carne with cheesy scones

Serves 4
Preparation time 30 minutes
Cooking time 55 minutes

scones
250 g (8 oz) plain flour
2 teaspoons baking powder
75 g (3 oz) butter, diced
50 g (2 oz) strong Cheddar cheese, grated
1 egg, beaten
50 ml (2 fl oz) milk

chilli con carne
415 g (13½ oz) **can Heinz Baked Beanz**
2 tablespoons light olive oil
1 onion, finely chopped
2 garlic cloves, crushed
500 g (1 lb) minced beef
2 tablespoons tomato purée
2 large red chillies, chopped
1 teaspoon hot chilli powder
2 teaspoons dried mixed herbs
400 g (13 oz) can chopped tomatoes

to serve
200 ml (7 fl oz) soured cream
2 tablespoons chopped flat leaf parsley
125 g (4 oz) Cheddar cheese, grated
jalapeño peppers (optional)

1 Make the scones. In large bowl mix together the flour and baking powder. Rub in the butter and add the cheese. Make a well in the centre and pour in the egg and milk. Use a knife to mix the dough until it comes together.

2 Turn out the dough on to a lightly floured surface and roll it out to about 5 mm (¼ inch) thick. Cut out 8 rounds, each 5 cm (2 inches) across, and place them on a baking sheet. Brush the tops with a little milk and bake in a preheated oven, 200°C (400°F), Gas Mark 6, for 12 minutes or until they sound hollow when tapped.

3 Make the chilli. Heat the oil in a large pan, add the onion and garlic and cook over medium heat for 5 minutes or until softened. Increase the heat to high and add the minced beef. Fry, stirring, for 5 minutes or until browned all over. Stir in the tomato purée, chillies, chilli powder and mixed herbs and continue to cook for 5 minutes. Add the tomatoes and **Heinz Baked Beanz**, bring to the boil, cover and simmer for 30 minutes or until the beef is tender.

4 Transfer the chilli con carne to a serving bowl and top with soured cream. Garnish with chopped parsley and serve with the scones and separate bowls of grated cheese and jalapeño peppers.

Provençal beanie mussels

Serves 4 as a starter or 2 as a
main course
Preparation time 20 minutes
Cooking time 10 minutes

415 g (13½ oz) can Heinz Baked Beanz
2 tablespoons olive oil
4 shallots, sliced
3 garlic cloves, chopped
150 ml (¼ pint) white wine
3 tomatoes, roughly chopped
1 kg (2 lb) fresh mussels, cleaned
2 tablespoons chopped flat leaf parsley,
   to garnish
1 baguette, to serve

1 Heat the oil in a large saucepan and cook the shallots and garlic for 3–4 minutes or until they are softened.

2 Add the wine, tomatoes and **Heinz Baked Beanz** and bring the mixture to the boil. Add the mussels and cover the pan. Cook over a high heat for 3–5 minutes or until all the mussels have opened, shaking the pan frequently.

3 Divide the mussels and sauce among 4 serving bowls, discarding any shells that remain unopened. Garnish with parsley and serve with lots of warm French bread.

grilled baked bean oysters with prosciutto

Serves 4
Preparation time 20 minutes
Cooking time 7–8 minutes

415 g (13½ oz) can Heinz Baked Beanz
12 fresh oysters in half shells
2 tablespoons chopped basil leaves,
   plus extra leaves to serve
1 teaspoon Worcestershire sauce
6 thin slices of prosciutto
Champagne, to serve

1 Remove the oysters from the shells. Wash and dry the shells thoroughly and place them on a baking sheet. Mix together the **Heinz Baked Beanz**, basil and Worcestershire sauce and divide the mixture among the shells.

2 Cook the prosciutto under a preheated grill until crisp. Allow to cool slightly and break into shards.

3 Put the oysters back into their shells, arranging them over the bean mixture. Cook under a preheated grill for 2–3 minutes or until the beans have heated through and the oysters are cooked. Scatter over the shards of prosciutto and torn basil leaves. Serve immediately with glasses of chilled Champagne.

bean around the clock

Beans are one of the most versatile foods around and whether they are eaten alone or jazzed up and combined with other ingredients, they really can be enjoyed at any time of the day.

fastest meal in the west

One of the great things about baked beans is that they are so quick and easy to prepare – a couple of minutes in a saucepan or the microwave and dinner is ready.

Baked beans are also the ideal food for novice chefs. Even the most inexperienced cook can open a can and use a toaster – a fact that comforts many mothers when their children first leave home. Countless students have been packed off to college with enough baked beans to stock a convenience store and will quickly learn to prepare nutritious, wholesome meals that won't break the bank and will keep their mothers from worrying!

comfort cooking

The refrigerator may be bare but there is always a can of baked beans hiding away in the back of the cupboard. People seem to long for comfort food when they haven't been shopping for weeks and a can of beans supplies the perfect solution.

There's something very warm and comforting about stirring a pan of beans. If you have ever arrived back from a trip at some unsociable hour you will be well aware of that craving for a nice cup of tea and a plate of beans on toast!

bring on breakfast

Beans are perfect for the most important meal of the day, as their slow-releasing carbohydrates will keep you going until lunchtime. The classic bacon and eggs combo goes fantastically well with baked beans and it is easy to turn this into a healthy option by poaching the eggs and grilling the bacon. For a relaxing alternative weekend brunch try the recipe for Bean, Mushroom and Brie-filled Pancakes (see page 8).

spicy bean burgers

Makes 8 burgers
Preparation time 25 minutes,
plus chilling
Cooking time 18 minutes

415 g (13½ oz) can Heinz Baked Beanz
1 tablespoon light olive oil
1 small onion, finely chopped
2 garlic cloves, crushed
1 red pepper, deseeded
   and finely chopped
1 teaspoon crushed dried chilli
½ teaspoon cayenne pepper
1 teaspoon Tabasco sauce
500 g (1 lb) mashed potato
3 tablespoons chopped parsley
125 g (4 oz) fresh breadcrumbs
vegetable oil, for frying
pepper

to serve
8 crispy rolls
salad leaves
2 tomatoes, sliced
chilli sauce (optional)

1 Heat the oil in a nonstick frying pan and add the onion, garlic and red pepper. Cook over low-medium heat for 5 minutes or until cooked through but not coloured. Add the chilli, cayenne pepper and Tabasco sauce, cook for a further minute then remove from the heat. Leave to one side to cool.

2 Mix the onion mixture with the mashed potato, **Heinz Baked Beanz** and parsley. Season well with pepper. Mix together using a potato masher or fork until thoroughly combined. Divide into 8 equal portions and drop each one into a large bowl of breadcrumbs. Form into balls then flatten these slightly into burgers. Cover and chill for 30 minutes.

3 Heat a little oil in a shallow, nonstick frying pan and cook the bean burgers in batches for 3 minutes on each side or until heated through and slightly crisp. Drain well on kitchen paper.

4 Halve and toast the rolls. Top each base with salad leaves, slices of tomato and a burger and serve, accompanied with chilli sauce if wished.

billboard beans

Heinz Baked Beanz have enjoyed a full and varied public life. Advertising has helped to bring the bean into people's homes and created memorable catchphrases that have become part of popular culture.

the early ads

The first famous advertising drive was the 'Joy of Living' campaign, launched in 1927. Beans were the star and, unusually for the time, the fact that Heinz Baked Beans (as they were known then) were free from preservatives and artificial colouring was emphasized.

1927

Above A Beanz Meanz Heinz advert from 1967.

Above 'Joy of Living' advertising campaign, 1937.

Beanz Meanz Heinz

The most memorable baked beans campaign was devised and launched in 1967. Such was its success that it ran for years and became what is undoubtedly the most famous and recognizable advertising campaign of all time.

Unless you were born on Mars (or are too young to remember) you are probably aware of these three little words and the simple but catchy

1967

jingle that accompanied the television ads. Like many great ideas, this one was devised in a flash of inspiration over a couple of beers. The man behind the catchphrase was Maurice Drake, a copywriter at the agency Young & Rubicam. Lacking inspiration, Drake took his team to the pub for a few pints. While doodling and jotting down various ideas, this particular combination popped into his head. The rest is history.

The Beanz Meanz Heinz campaign was so successful that it ran for over 20 years, and the basic jingle was reworded and tweaked to create new ads. The original words to the jingle were:

'A million housewives every day, Open a can of beans and say, Beanz Meanz Heinz.'

Above 2004 'superbean' nutritional advert.

today's ads

Paying homage to the much-loved catchphrase, Heinz has changed the spelling of beans to 'beanz' in its most recent advertising campaign, reminding people how good baked beans are for you.

Humble they may be, but still very much deserving of the label 'superbean'. Over the years, Heinz Baked Beanz have become such an iconic brand that they are now firmly embedded in our culture. Not many brands can claim to have had such an impact on the nation's eating habits, and they are as popular today as they ever were.

43

bean and red pepper sushi

Makes 24
Preparation time 35 minutes,
plus cooling
Cooking time 22 minutes

415 g (13½ oz) can Heinz Baked Beanz
400 g (13 oz) sushi rice
2 tablespoons caster sugar
good pinch of salt
75 ml (3 fl oz) rice vinegar
4 sheets nori
2 teaspoons wasabi
3 tablespoons chopped coriander
1 teaspoon Thai fish sauce
½ red pepper, deseeded
   and cut into thin strips

to serve
soy sauce
pickled ginger

1 Rinse the rice under cold running water. Put the rice in a heavy-based saucepan with 600 ml (1 pint) water. Bring to the boil, cover and cook over low heat for 12 minutes. Remove the pan from the heat and leave, covered, for 10 minutes.

2 Stir together the sugar, salt and vinegar until the sugar dissolves. Spread the rice over a non-metallic sheet and use a spatula to fold the vinegar dressing through it, gently separating the grains of rice as you fold. Spread a damp tea towel over the rice and leave to cool to room temperature.

3 Put a sheet of nori, shiny side down, on a sushi mat. Spread the rice to a depth of about 1 cm (½ inch) over the nori, leaving a 1 cm (½ inch) border at the top and bottom. Make a shallow groove horizontally across the rice and spread a small amount of wasabi along the groove.

4 Mix together the **Heinz Baked Beanz**, coriander and Thai fish sauce and spread 3–4 tablespoons over the rice leaving a margin of 5 cm (2 inches) at the top and bottom of the rice. Arrange some of the red pepper strips across the rice. Use the mat to roll up the sushi. Use a sharp knife to trim the ends and cut the roll into 6 pieces. Repeat with the other nori sheets. Serve the sushi immediately with soy sauce and pickled ginger in separate bowls.

chicken and bean cassoulet with chorizo

Serves 4
Preparation time 15 minutes
Cooking time 40 minutes

415 g (13½ oz) can Heinz Baked Beanz
1 tablespoon olive oil
4 raw chorizo sausages
1 large red onion, roughly chopped
2 large chicken breasts,
   each cut into 4 pieces
400 g (13 oz) can chopped tomatoes
300 g (10 oz) can butter beans
3 sprigs of thyme

to serve
mashed potatoes
sprigs of thyme

1 Heat the oil in a large, nonstick frying pan. Add the chorizo sausages and cook for 4–5 minutes over medium heat or until lightly browned all over. Transfer the sausages to a plate and use the fat remaining in the pan to cook the onion and chicken for 5 minutes or until the chicken has browned and the onions have softened.

2 Cut each sausage into 2–3 pieces and return them to the pan. Stir in the tomatoes, **Heinz Baked Beanz**, butter beans and thyme sprigs. Bring the mixture to the boil, cover and cook over a low heat for 25–30 minutes or until the meat is cooked and the sauce has thickened.

3 Serve the cassoulet spooned over freshly mashed potato and garnished with sprigs of thyme.

bean around the world

Heinz Baked Beanz are now sold in a staggering 61 countries around the world. The recipes in this book reflect their global appeal, with inspiration taken from Italy, Morocco, India and the US to name but a few.

beans in all cuisines

One of the reasons why Heinz Baked Beanz have proved to be such a hit around the world is that many countries have a rich culinary history that includes many different varieties of beans. As a great source of protein and carbohydrates, beans are an excellent choice for hearty meals and you will find beans popping up in all kinds of dishes, such as chickpeas or split peas in Indian dishes and black beans in Caribbean cooking.

stateside beans

Many Americans enjoy eating Heinz Baked Beanz, although this is more likely to be beans with steak, burgers or waffles than beans on toast. First produced in the country in 1895, the US version is made to a different recipe, which is why you will find both Heinz American and English Baked Beans in the US.

Above A British Heinz Baked Beanz can.

Canadian beans

With a maple leaf on the national flag, it seems natural to include a maple syrup version among the Canadian Baked Beans. Maple-Style Beans with Pure Quebec Maple Syrup, and Deep Brown Beans with Pork Molasses are just two varieties that have proved to be big hits in Canada.

bean down under

Beans have been exported to Australia since the beginning of the last century and the first Aussie-made baked beans were rolling off the conveyor belts from 1935. As well as the classic British version, a number of variations have been a big hit with bean fans. These include Baked Beans in Ham Sauce, and Baked Beans with Meatballs.

a trip to China

Heinz products have been available in China since 1990. Beans have proved to be such a hit that they are regularly served in the restaurant at the Olympic Sports Training Centre in Beijing, where athletes are preparing for the next Olympics.

Above A Chinese billboard advertising Heinz Baked Beanz.

rushing to Russia

Russia is one of the most recent converts to baked beans as they have only been exported there since 1996. There was a modest prediction for sales but it seems that the Russians are smitten with the new arrival on the supermarket shelves – they consumed 50 per cent more than predicted and extra beans had to be ordered to keep up with demand!

bean international

Today Heinz Baked Beanz have a truly international appeal and are sold in 69 countries, including, to name but a few, India, Africa, Hong Kong and the Middle East.

49

Moroccan bean and lamb tagine

Serves 4
Preparation time 20 minutes,
plus marinating
Cooking time 2 hours 10
minutes

415 g (13½ oz) can Heinz Baked Beanz
1 teaspoon cumin seeds
1 teaspoon coriander seeds
grated rind of 1 orange
2 tablespoons olive oil
2 garlic cloves, crushed
2 onions, cut into wedges
750 g (1½ lb) lamb, cut into large cubes
400 g (13 oz) can chopped tomatoes
125 ml (4 fl oz) red wine
1 tablespoon clear honey
1 cinnamon stick
125 g (4 oz) ready-to-eat dried apricots

to serve
250 g (8 oz) couscous
3 tablespoons chopped mint
grated rind and juice of 1 lemon
25 g (1 oz) roasted flaked almonds
lemon wedges

1 Make the marinade. Heat the cumin and coriander seeds in a small, nonstick frying pan over medium heat until they start to smoke. Remove the pan from the heat and leave to cool. Grind the seeds using a pestle and mortar.

2 Mix together the ground spices, orange rind, oil, garlic and onions. Mix the cubed lamb in the marinade until it is completed coated, cover and leave to marinate overnight.

3 Heat a large, nonstick frying pan and cook the lamb, in batches, until it is browned all over. Transfer the meat to a large, heavy-based pan. Add the tomatoes, wine, honey and cinnamon stick and stir to mix. Bring the mixture to the boil, cover and cook over a low heat for 2 hours or until the lamb is tender. Add the **Heinz Baked Beanz** and apricots to the pan and cook for a further 10 minutes.

4 Meanwhile, prepare the couscous according to the instructions on the packet and stir through the mint, lemon juice and rind. Serve the tagine over the couscous. Sprinkle with flaked almonds and garnish with a wedge of lemon.

Heinz bean editions

While the original Baked Beanz will always be a family favourite, Heinz have made some exciting and popular additions to the classic beans in tomato sauce.

Ideal for those who love beans but are health-conscious too.

The original and best, Heinz Baked Beanz are loved worldwide.

Kids can't get enough of this store-cupboard staple.

baked beanz with cumberland sausages

This meal-in-a-tin is great with a traditional cooked breakfast.

mean beanz

Spice up your life with the hot new Mean Beanz range.

baked beanz with lea & perrins

Limited edition Heinz Baked Beanz with Lea & Perrins – perfect!

cheesy cod and bean tarts

Makes 6
Preparation time 30 minutes,
plus chilling
Cooking time 30 minutes

415 g (13½ oz) can Heinz Baked Beanz
200 g (7 oz) plain flour
pinch of salt
125 g (4 oz) butter
5 tablespoons grated Parmesan cheese
300 g (10 oz) cod fillet, skinned and boned
50 g (2 oz) fresh breadcrumbs
2 tablespoons chopped parsley

1 Place the flour, salt, 100 g (3½ oz) butter and 3 tablespoons Parmesan in a food processor and blend until the mixture resembles fine breadcrumbs. Transfer to a large bowl and add 6–7 tablespoons chilled water. Bring the mixture together with your fingertips to form a soft dough. Chill for 30 minutes.

2 Roll out the pastry on a lightly floured surface and use it to line 6 lightly greased tart tins, each 10 cm (4 inches) across. Chill for 30 minutes. Line the tins with baking paper and fill with baking beans. Bake blind in a preheated oven, 180°C (350°F), Gas Mark 4, for 15 minutes. Remove the paper and baking beans and return the tarts to the oven for 5 minutes.

3 Steam the cod over a pan of simmering water for 5 minutes until it is cooked through. Break the fish into flakes and carefully combine the flakes of fish with the **Heinz Baked Beanz**. Use the mixture to fill the precooked tarts cases.

4 Make the topping. Melt the remaining butter in a frying pan and gently fry the breadcrumbs for 2–3 minutes until they are light golden in colour. Add the parsley and remaining Parmesan and spoon the mixture over the top of the tarts. Cook for 10–15 minutes until the top is golden and the filling starts to bubble around the sides.

Christmas bean and turkey pies

Makes 8
Preparation time 20 minutes
Cooking time 35 minutes

415 g (13½ oz) can Heinz Baked Beanz
150 g (5 oz) cooked turkey, chopped or
   shredded into bite-sized pieces
2 tablespoons cranberry sauce,
   plus extra to serve
1 teaspoon Worcestershire sauce
500 g (1 lb) shortcrust pastry
   (thawed if frozen)
1 egg yolk, beaten, for glazing
pepper
green salad, to serve

1 In a medium-sized bowl mix together the **Heinz Baked Beanz**, turkey, cranberry sauce and Worcestershire sauce. Season with pepper and leave to one side.

2 Roll out the pastry on a lightly floured surface and cut out 8 rounds, each 12 cm (5 inches) across. Use the rounds to line a lightly greased 8-hole muffin tin, leaving a slight overhang of pastry. Divide the filling among the pastry cases. Re-roll the remaining pastry and cut out 6 rounds, each 8 cm (3 inches) across. Brush the overhanging pastry with a little water, place the lids on top and press down the edges to seal.

3 Brush the tops of the pies with beaten egg yolk and make a small hole in the top of each. Bake in a preheated oven, 180°C (350°F), Gas Mark 4, for 35 minutes until golden-brown. Serve warm with a little green salad and extra cranberry sauce.

ten ways with toast

There is nothing quicker or easier to prepare than a plate of baked beans on toast. We've picked ten deliciously different ways to prepare your favourite snack.

classic beanz on toast

Put the Heinz Baked Beanz in a pan and heat, stirring constantly. Toast the bread then butter and pour over the beans. Pleasure on a plate!

bacon and bean bagel

Heat the Heinz Baked Beanz in a pan and grill 2 rashers of bacon. Add a couple of shakes of Worcestershire sauce and toast the bagel halves under the grill. Butter the bagel liberally, top with the bacon rashers and pour over the beans.

sunday brunch beanz

Chop 2 rashers of smoky bacon and fry in a pan. Add 1 chopped flat mushroom, stir for a minute or two then add the Heinz Baked Beanz. Sprinkle over a few drops of Worcestershire sauce. Toast the bread, butter liberally and pour over the beans. Sprinkle over some freshly chopped parsley.

chilli beanz

Fry half a chopped green pepper, one-quarter of a chopped red onion and a little fresh green chilli. Add the Heinz Baked Beanz and heat through. Toast 2 slices of bread. Butter the toast and pour over the beans.

rustic beanz

Fry 50 g (2 oz) chopped chorizo. Add some chopped onion and a chopped garlic clove. Empty a can of

Heinz BBQ Beanz into the pan and heat through. Toast two slices of bread and pour over the beans.

cheesy beanz

Prepare the Heinz Baked Beans as above. Grate a good wedge of cheese into a bowl. Pour the beans on the toast, sprinkle over the grated cheese and allow it to melt into the piping hot beans.

gallic beanz

Halve a small baguette lengthways and toast one half under a preheated grill. Heat the Heinz Baked Beanz in a pan and grate some Emmental cheese. Pour the beans over the baguette, top with the grated cheese and place under the grill for 1–2 minutes, until the cheese has melted.

some like it hot

Heat the Heinz Baked Beanz in a pan, add a few drops of Tabasco sauce and a little chopped fresh chilli. Toast two slices of bread. Butter the toast and pour over the beans.

tipsy beanz

Empty the Heinz Baked Beanz into a pan and heat. Add a dash of red wine and stir. Grate a little Parmesan and mix with a sprinkling of breadcrumbs and some chopped parsley. Toast a waffle then spread with butter and pour over the beans. Sprinkle the breadcrumb mix over the beans then place under a preheated grill for 1–2 minutes to allow the topping to melt and brown.

fancy beanz

Heat the Heinz Baked Beanz in a pan. Crack an egg and poach in a pan of simmering water. Split an English muffin, toast it then spread with butter. Pour the beans over the muffin, place the poached egg on top and top with a small spoon of crème fraîche. Finish with a sprinkle of freshly chopped chives.

spiced shepherd's pie

Serves 4
Preparation time 25 minutes
Cooking time 1¼ hours

filling
415 g (13½ oz) can Heinz Baked Beanz
1 tablespoon light olive oil
1 onion, chopped
1 small carrot, chopped
1 green chilli, deseeded and chopped
2 teaspoons curry powder
2 teaspoons black mustard seeds
500 g (1 lb) minced lamb
2 tablespoons mango chutney
100 ml (3½ fl oz) meat stock

topping
1 kg (2 lb) potatoes, cut into quarters
50 g (2 oz) butter
25 g (1 oz) Cheddar cheese, grated
1 green chilli, finely sliced
1 teaspoon black mustard seeds
salt and pepper

1 Heat the oil in an ovenproof frying pan. Add the onion, carrot, chilli, curry powder and mustard seeds and cook over medium heat for 5 minutes. Turn the heat to high and add the lamb. Fry, stirring, for 5 minutes until the meat is browned all over. Stir in the chutney, **Heinz Baked Beanz** and stock. Continue to cook for 5 minutes until the sauce has thickened. Leave to one side to cool slightly.

2 Make the topping. Cook the potatoes in salted boiling water for 25 minutes until soft. Drain well and mash with the butter. Season with salt and pepper and spoon the mashed potato over the lamb. Sprinkle the cheese, chilli and mustard seeds over the potato and bake in a preheated oven, 200°C (400°F), Gas Mark 6, for 30–35 minutes until the pie is golden on top and the filling is bubbling around the sides.

bean and potato pizza

Serves 4
Preparation time 35 minutes,
plus proving
Cooking time 15 minutes

415 g (13½ oz) can Heinz Baked Beanz
500 g (1 lb) strong bread or pizza flour
1 teaspoon salt
7 g (¼ oz) sachet easy-blend dried yeast
4 tablespoons olive oil
1 large potato, thinly sliced
1 garlic clove, crushed
3 tablespoons chopped rosemary
4 tablespoons grated pecorino cheese
salt and pepper

1 Make the pizza base. In a large bowl mix together the flour, salt and yeast and make a well in the centre. Pour 300 ml (½ pint) lukewarm water into the well and add 1 tablespoon oil. Gradually work in the flour to form a soft but not sticky dough. Turn out on to a lightly floured surface and knead for 5 minutes until the dough is elastic and smooth. Transfer to a clean bowl, cover with clingfilm and a damp cloth and leave to rise at room temperature for about 1 hour or until the dough has doubled in size.

2 Knock back the dough and divide it into 4 pieces. Roll out one piece on a lightly floured surface to a round 30 cm (12 inches) across. Place on a floured baking sheet. Repeat with the remaining dough to make 4 rounds in all.

3 Lightly mash the **Heinz Baked Beanz** with the back of a fork and spread them over the pizza bases. Top each base with the thinly sliced potato. Mix together the remaining olive oil and crushed garlic and drizzle over the potatoes. Scatter over the rosemary and pecorino. Season to taste with salt and pepper and bake in a preheated oven, 220°C (425°F), Gas Mark 7, for 15 minutes or until the potatoes have coloured slightly and are cooked through. Serve immediately.

quirky bean facts

Not only are Heinz Baked Beanz a superfood and a nutritional part of everyday life, they also have a fun and quirky side.

brits and beans

- The Brits eat the most cans of baked beans per person in the world.
- Beans are often taken on expeditions – Captain Scott himself even ate them in the Antarctic.
- Between 1941 and 1948, the Ministry of Food gave baked beans an 'essential food' classification as part of the wartime rationing system.

Above An alternative use for beans!

- The first can of baked beans was sold in Fortnum & Mason in 1901. At that time, beans were seen as a luxury food item and cost the equivalent of £1.50 at today's prices.

Above F.J. Hooper eating beans on Scott's British Antarctic Expedition, 1910–1913.

- Heinz Baked Bean Pizza was launched in 1995 to celebrate the centenary of Heinz Baked Beanz.

number-crunching

- Heinz sells 1.5 million cans of beans every day.
- The can-making centre at Kitt Green produces more than one billion cans every year.
- Heinz uses enough tomatoes to fill an Olympic-

- sized swimming pool every day.
- Baked beans are exported to 61 countries around the world.
- 451 million cans of baked beans are consumed in Britain every year.
- Half a standard size can of baked beans counts as one of your five daily portions of fruit and veg.

- Boston has the nickname 'Bean Town' due to its namesake recipe Boston Baked Beans.
- 6 January is National Bean Day in America.
- The navy bean is the official vegetable of Massachusetts.

- Beans made an appearance on the album cover of The Who's 'The Who Sell Out'. Roger Daltrey can be seen lying in a bath filled with beans while

Above The Who's album cover.

holding a giant Heinz Baked Beans can.
- Australian cricketer Shane Warne loves Heinz Baked Beanz so much that he takes them on tour.

Above Cricketer Shane Warne.

- When the Argentinean football player, Gabriel Ivan Heinze, signed for Manchester United in 2004, he requested 57 as his squad number.
- Guinness world record attempts featuring baked beans include: flicking baked beans from a bath into a bucket; eating as many baked beans as possible in one minute using a cocktail stick; and sitting in a bath of baked beans for as long as possible.
- In 1998 Heinz Baked Beanz was selected as one of the brands that people thought represented the final ten years of the millennium.
- And in 2005 Heinz Baked Beans were voted 'Most Loved Brand' by the British public.

index

acknowledgements

Executive Editor Sarah Ford

Editor Emma Pattison

Executive Art Editor Darren Southern

Picture Researcher Emma O'Neil

Additional Picture Research
David Thomas and Chloe Veale at
The History of Advertising Trust Archive

Production Manager Ian Paton

Special photography © Octopus Publishing Group Limited/Lis Parsons.

Heinz Beans can photography © Octopus Publishing Group Limited/Andy Komorowski.

Other photography: Alamy/Royal Geographical Society/Herbert Ponting 62 bottom.**Corbis UK Ltd**/Bettmann 12. **Mark Farrell** 38. **Getty Images**/Ryan Pierse 63 top. **H J Heinz historical collection, held at, and preserved by,**

The History of Advertising Trust Archive. (www.hatads.org.uk) 4, 5 bottom, 6, 7, 13, 14, 15, 18, 32, 42 top and bottom; /Photograph by Snowden, Camera Press, London 25 top. **HJ Heinz** 29, 43, 52 centre and right, 53. **Library and Archives Division, Historical Society of Western Pennsylvania, Pittsburgh,** 19. **Mirrorpix** 33. **Rex Features**/Jones (SEN) 49; /Organic Picture Library 52 left. **TopFoto**/PA 49; /Jaime Turner 62 top.